Duluth

ACKNOWLEDGEMENTS:

For Ellen and John for their love and encouragement.
And for Tim for bringing me to Duluth and for sharing his
exuberance in all things natural and historical.

PREFACE:

My first memory of Duluth was seeing a glimpse of twinkling lights on a hillside with the antenna farm scattered along the top of the hill. My husband and I were driving north from Illinois one summer evening on Highway 53 south of Superior, Wisconsin. We were on our way to go canoeing in the Boundary Waters. Tim explained we were crossing the ancient beach of a long ago glacial lake. You have to be quick or you might miss this peek of Duluth as you come north. Now that we have lived here for over 20 years the view we are even more thrilled to see is when we return to Duluth on Interstate 35 coming north over Thompson Hill and we see the St. Louis River Valley as it flows into Lake Superior. It is like sighing over fireworks displays on the Fourth of July. Even in mysterious fog there is a sense of awe as we descend into the Twin Ports. It has been a great place to live and raise a family. We think Duluth is a very special place.

PHOTO CREDITS AND COPYRIGHT OWNERS:

Cover: Dan Grandmaison, Grandmaison Photographic Studios
Sam Alvar, Seaquest Commercial Photography: 32, 46, 99 (top) **Joel Bahma:** 118 **Dudley Edmondson, Raptor Works:** 5, 16, 22, 59 (bottom), 66, 67 (both), 72, 85 (top), 90, 96, 97 (top), 102, 109 (bottom), 110, 111 (both), 112, 113 (bottom) **Brett Groehler, UMD:** 75, 77 (top), 82, 101 (top), 103, back cover (bottom) **Bill Lindner Photography:** 23 (top), 113 (top) **William J. Midbrod:** 44 (top) **Ken Newhams, Duluth Shipping News:** 35 (bottom), 44 (bottom), 45 (bottom), 115 (top), 117 (top) **Dennis O'Hara, Northern Images Photography:** 6, 48, 68, 116, 122 **Mike Peterson:** 119 **Stan Tekiela:** 61 (bottom), 83, 93 (bottom), 94 (both), 95 (middle), 101 (bottom) **John Zager:** 50 (top), 55 **Tim Zager:** all other photos

Book and Cover Design by Jonathan Norberg

10 9 8 7 6 5 4 3 2

Copyright 2004 by Anita Zager
Published by Adventure Publications, Inc.
820 Cleveland Street South
Cambridge, MN 55008
1-800-678-7006
www.adventurepublications.net

ISBN-13: 978-1-59193-054-9
ISBN-10: 1-59193-054-5

Duluth
GEM OF THE FRESHWATER SEA

By Anita Zager

ADVENTURE PUBLICATIONS, INC.
CAMBRIDGE, MN

TABLE OF CONTENTS

Introduction 7
Headwaters of the Inland Seas 11
Lake Superior 13
Old Rock 15
St. Louis River 17
    Jay Cooke State Park 17
Natural Harbor 21
Fond du Lac—Ojibwe Ancestors 23
Early Europeans 25
Early Development 27
Great Water Highway 29
    Portages 30
Duluth Ship Canal 33
The Aerial Lift Bridge 37
Sailing Vessels 41
Weather 43
Shipwrecks 47
Lighthouses 49
    Duluth Port Entry Lights 51
The North Shore 53
    Split Rock Lighthouse 53
    Two Harbors Lighthouse 53
    Ore Docks at Two Harbors 54
    Gooseberry Falls State Park 54
Commercial Fishing 57
Ship Building 59
Iron Ore 61
Railroading 63
Lumber 67
Modern Shipping 69
Aviation 73
Education 75
    University of Minnesota Duluth 75
    College of St. Scholastica 76
    University of Wisconsin Superior 76
Regional Medical Center 79
    St. Luke's 79
    St. Mary's/Duluth Clinic and the Miller-Dwan Medical Center 79
Architectural Landmarks 81
    Old Duluth Central High School 81
    The Depot/St. Louis County Heritage & Arts Center 81
    Glensheen 82
    Fitger's 82
    First United Methodist Church 84
    Duluth Public Library 85
    Kitchi Gammi Club 85
    Henry H. Meyers House 86
    Arthur P. Cook House 86
    Observation Hill 86

Diverse Community 89
Public Sculpture 91
Attractions 93
    Lake Superior Zoo 93
    Lake Superior Maritime Visitor Center 93
    S.S. William A. Irvin Ore Boat Museum and the *Lake Superior* Tugboat 94
    Vista Fleet 94
    Great Lakes Aquarium 94
    U.S. Coast Guard Cutter *Sundew* 95
    Lake Superior Railroad Museum and the North Shore Scenic Railroad 95
Canal Park 97
Downtown Lakewalk 99
    Bayfront Festival Park 99
Arts Scene 101
    The Depot/St. Louis County Heritage & Arts Center 101
    Sacred Heart Music Center 101
    Weber Music Hall 101
    Duluth Entertainment and Convention Center 101
    Tweed Museum of Art at UMD 102
    Coffeehouse and Gallery Scene 102
    Theater and Dance 102
Parks & Natural Areas 105
    Enger Tower 105
    Skyline Parkway 105
    The Willard Munger State Trail 105
    Leif Erickson Park 106
    Rose Garden 106
Superior, Wisconsin 109
    Fairlawn Mansion 109
    Trails Galore 109
    Barker's Island 110
    Richard I. Bong WWII Heritage Center 110
    Superior Port Entry 110
Spring in Duluth 113
Summer in Duluth 115
Fall in Duluth 117
Winter in Duluth 119
Conclusion 123

Introduction

The story of Duluth must begin with its geologic history, and how the waters of Lake Superior and the St. Louis River met after the great Ice Age to form a unique natural harbor. The Great Lakes have been a major water highway connecting the interior of the country to the Atlantic Ocean, with Lake Superior as the headwaters of the Lakes, and Duluth as the major port. The St. Louis River, which connects northern Minnesota's interior with the Duluth harbor, also became part of the water route. An important junction along this route was the Native American settlement of Fond du Lac, at the most western edge of Duluth. Located right on the St. Louis River, this settlement was instrumental in transporting traded furs and goods up and down the river into Lake Superior. This water highway also brought the French trappers and explorers, including Duluth's namesake, Daniel Greysolon Du Lhut (Sieur Du Lhut), and eventually thousands of immigrants.

Transportation is always vital to the economic success of a community and this was no different for Duluth and Superior. With the digging of a canal, the discovery of iron ore, and the building of railroads, ships and docks, modern day Duluth continues to adapt to changing times. Duluth, always home to visionary entrepreneurs, is now home to several important medical facilities and educational institutions.

The city limits of Duluth are quite unusual. Following the ridgeline of the ancient shoreline and spanning 25 miles, the limits can be marked from Fond du Lac and the St. Louis River in the west to the Lester River in the east. Many streams cascade down the hillside forming excellent forested highways for northland animals that can suddenly find themselves in the middle of a city with 87,000 people. There are over 11,000 acres of open and wooded land, 20 miles of hiking trails and 23 city parks.

In the mid 1850s approximately eleven town sites were platted in the present city limits. By 1859, one by one, they had become incorporated into the city of Duluth. Some of these

Retired tugboat, *Lake Superior*

Looking east from Skyline Parkway above downtown Duluth

continue to be recognized as unique neighborhoods within the larger community and Duluthians are proud of these neighborhoods.

While Northern Minnesota's rugged landscape and erratic, even extreme weather conditions might not appeal to some, others are irresistibly drawn to its dramatic, distinct seasons and multitude of activities unique for a city its size. Many organizations first formed at the height of Duluth's economic history continue to support vibrant educational, fine art and civic groups that make life in Duluth so rich.

Written for a fuller understanding of Duluth and its diversity of citizens, this book celebrates how the city came to be and how it finds its current form.

Central Hillside seen from the Ship Canal

View from Thompson Hill Visitor Center

By the twentieth century, Duluth had grown into a major port that connected the middle of the continent to the Atlantic.

Headwaters of the Inland Seas

Many great cities have been built on bodies of water. Even so, Duluth's setting is special. It is located in the middle of the North American continent at the westernmost point of the world's largest chain of freshwater seas. The backdrop of the steep hills against a foreground of an incredible body of water sets the stage for an interesting story.

A few facts about Duluth:

Population: 86,000

Population within a 30-mile radius: 184,000

Via the St. Lawrence Seaway, it is 2,342 freshwater miles from the Atlantic Ocean

Altitude ranges from 605 feet at Lake Superior's shoreline to 1,485 feet at the ridgeline

The city limits reach 30 miles long by 6 miles wide

Duluth has more than 11,000 acres of wooded and open land, 20 miles of hiking trails and 23 parks

Steep hills of Duluth

Downtown Duluth

Lake Superior

Lake Superior appears on the maps and in the journals of early French explorers as *le lac superieur*, meaning upper lake. At its eastern shore, Lake Superior empties into Lake Huron via the rapids of the St. Marys River at Sault Ste. Marie, Michigan. Water then flows south toward Detroit into Lake Erie, spills into Lake Ontario via the Welland Ship Canal at Niagara Falls, enters the St. Lawrence River and finally pours into the Atlantic Ocean at the Gulf of St. Lawrence.

Lake Superior is large enough to contain all the other Great Lakes, plus three more the size of Lake Erie. It is the largest freshwater lake in the world by surface area (31,700 square miles) and contains approximately ten percent of Earth's fresh water. Its average temperature is 40° F. Lake Superior's vast surface area of cold water creates notorious weather of its own; lake effect precipitation brings heavy rain and snow, and storms over history have strewn its depths with more than 350 shipwrecks. The Lake measures 350 miles east to west and 160 miles north to south. It has an average depth of 483 feet; its deepest point is 1,333 feet. Its retention, or replacement time, is 191 years. It joins the middle of North America to the Atlantic Ocean via the St. Lawrence Seaway, which passes through the Atlantic provinces of Canada. It has 1,400 islands and shoals. Evidence of human activity in the region extends back at least 9,000 years.

Ship arriving in early winter

Lake Superior's North Shore

Old Rock

Whether a visitor first approaches Duluth over the high, rocky ridges of Thompson Hill from the west, or across the prehistoric beaches of Glacial Lake Duluth south of Superior, Wisconsin, the beautiful geologic formations that make up Lake Superior's western shore never fail to impress. Some of the oldest exposed rock in North America (2.7 billion years old) is found in northern Minnesota. Every corner in the Twin Ports of Duluth and Superior bears examples of the ancient phenomena that created the area's distinctive topography.

Great views of the topography can be had at Hawk Ridge at the eastern end of Duluth's Skyline Parkway. A plaque at this location gives an excellent description of Glacial Lake Duluth. From this viewpoint, it is possible to observe the slope of the land and the ancient beach, now Wisconsin's shoreline.

Just west of Duluth, Jay Cooke State Park is another great place to observe some of the results of the area's geologic history. Ancient lava flows and huge near-vertical slabs of slate are just a pair of the sights to enjoy.

Rock picking is a popular pastime for young and old alike. The Lake Superior Agate is a particularly prized stone that can be found on the rocky beaches of the North Shore and at inland quarries. Lake Superior Agates were formed by dissolved silica that percolated through gas pockets in old lava beds.

Rocky outcrop downtown

Rocky North Shore beach

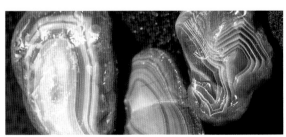
Lake Superior Agates

St. Louis River

The St. Louis River, which drains a large portion of northeastern Minnesota, is Lake Superior's largest American tributary. It begins its major cascade into Lake Superior just outside Carlton, Minnesota, and is one of many rivers that flow over the jagged rock hillsides of Duluth. Motorists can get great views of the river from Highway 210 in Jay Cooke State Park. Visitors can hike the volcanic folds along the riverbed or observe the tilted slabs of slate from the famous Swinging Bridge, which spans the river near the park's visitor center. The bottom of the St. Louis River Portage, called Knife Portage after the tilted slabs of slate, is the site of Fond du Lac, the earliest human encampment in Duluth.

As the river makes its way to Lake Superior, it passes through sandstone formations near the Fond du Lac neighborhood of western Duluth. In this same area, the Wisconsin bank of the river begins to exhibit the red clay and sand deposited by Glacial Lake Duluth. This area is also marked by numerous islands and bays. The St. Louis River picks up sediment and silt and deposits it to form Minnesota Point in Lake Superior, the largest natural sandbar in the world. The river's natural outlet passes through what is now the Superior Port Entry, and also marks the state line between Minnesota and Wisconsin. Its outlet is marked by the Wisconsin Point Lighthouse.

Tilted slabs of slate at Jay Cooke State Park

Jay Cooke State Park

Land along the St. Louis River was donated in 1915 to develop Jay Cooke State Park.

The Swinging Bridge and log and stone buildings were constructed as part of the Civilian Conservation Corps (CCC) projects in the 1930s and early 1940s.

Jay Cooke State Park helps to preserve important features and histories of the area. The geological features, so important in the area's history and development, are protected and valued here. Jay Cooke State Park also preserves part of the history of

Swinging Bridge at Jay Cooke State Park

the area's earliest inhabitants, who were able to thrive because the waterways provided access to seasonal hunting, gathering and fur trapping grounds. In its name, this state park honors the legacy of Jay Cooke, a railroad baron who overcame the area's geological barriers to build his transcontinental railroad to the West Coast.

West Duluth neighborhoods along St. Louis River

Banks of the St. Louis River

Natural Harbor

The twin ports of Duluth and Superior are nestled in a natural harbor at the western end of Lake Superior. Minnesota Point, the largest natural sandbar in the world, provides an effective breakwater that was valued as much by early navigators as it is today.

As the ocean-going ships approach the harbor, special navigation pilots come aboard to help the crews safely and precisely guide the ships through the canal and channels to their berths. The waterfront of the Twin Ports is about 49 miles long with 17 miles of dredged channels.

Minnesota Point beach

Minnesota Point, world's largest sandbar

Fond du Lac—Ojibwe Ancestors

Evidence indicates that Native Americans have had a presence in this region since approximately 7,000 BC. Various ancestral groups moved through the region from both the west and the east. The classic water routes brought the Ojibwe along the St. Lawrence River through Sault Ste. Marie "to La Pointe on Madeline Island, the great homeland of the Ojibwe people." Madeline Island (near Bayfield, WI) was their spiritual home for 120 years, before it was suddenly abandoned. At that time, many bands moved north, south and west to settle in parts of Canada, Michigan, Wisconsin and Minnesota.

As fur trade developed, shifts occurred among the various Native American groups of the Great Lakes region. The Dakota moved into the woodlands and plains of western Minnesota as the Ojibwe pushed west and north as a result of pressure from the Iroquois in the east. The Ojibwe controlled much of the region by around 1700.

In the 1600s, French explorers and missionaries established contact with Native Americans. A vibrant fur trade developed, and for a period of time, generally positive relationships grew between the French and Native Americans. This era was marked by several important events, such as the contribution of Father Baraga's dictionary of the Ojibwe language.

The Ojibwe encampment at Fond du Lac was part of an important trading network that included villages at La Pointe on Madeline Island, Grand Portage, MN, and Bois Forte on Lake Vermilion. On September 15, 1679, Daniel Greysolon, Sieur du Lhut met at Fond du Lac with representatives of the Native American nations to convince the various groups to live peacefully among each other so that trade could prosper and benefit them all. Over the years the economic importance of the fur trade grew and John Jacob Astor established an American Fur Company Post at Fond du Lac in the early 1800s. But by the 1840s the fur trade in Minnesota collapsed. The La Pointe Treaty of 1854 ceded the entire Minnesota shoreline of Lake Superior to the United States and ushered in a new era.

Harvesting wild rice

Voyager Rendezvous reenactment at Old Fort William

Early Europeans

French explorers came in contact with the Dakota and Ojibwe as early as 1612. Jean Nicolet recorded his first contact with the Dakota in 1639. French Jesuits reached Lake Superior in 1640 and found the summer camps of the Ojibwe at Sault Ste. Marie. The French explorers and missionaries thoroughly explored the length of the Mississippi and its connections to the Great Lakes Region.

Communities and enterprises throughout the region bear the names of these early European visitors (Groseilliers, Radisson, Menard, Marquette, La Salle).

Father Hennepin, a Franciscan friar, was traveling north along the Mississippi in 1679–80 when he was apprehended by the Dakota, brought north and held along with other members of his party at Lake Mille Lacs.

Grand Portage National Monument

Daniel Greysolon, Sieur du Lhut, arrived in the western part of Lake Superior from Montreal in 1679–1680 and was able to convince the Dakota to release Hennepin in June of 1680 as a part of a peace negotiation among the tribes of the region west of Lake Superior. The goal of the treaty was to create a peaceful trading environment in which the fur trade between the native people and the French trading companies could prosper. Du Lhut, like many explorers of the era, hoped to discover the route to the Pacific Ocean.

Gradually British and American fur companies challenged the French to establish their own trading posts. Thus began the struggle for economic and political domination of the region. With the 1763 Treaty of Paris, the French forfeited their territory claims east of the Mississippi to the British, who then held that territory until after the War of 1812. The brisk fur trade eventually depleted the animal resources of the area. When trapping played out, other enterprises became important.

Lester Park Rendezvous reenactment

Early Development

During the early years of development, a collection of settlements or villages emerged along Duluth's waterfront from west to east. Gradually, these communities became incorporated into the City of Duluth. Many of Duluth's neighborhoods are still known by their original village names: Fond du Lac, Rice's Point, Minnesota Point, Portland, Endion. Other neighborhoods are named for the various rivers and streams that flow through them: Chester Park, Congdon Park, Lester Park, Lincoln Park. Morgan Park in western Duluth was actually a planned community designed for the employees of the U.S. Steel mill. The topography of the area required the city to have a long and narrow arrangement along the hillside, so many of the original neighborhoods have managed to preserve their unique identities.

Early archival pictures show scraggly assortments of clapboard buildings in clearings dotted with tree stumps. The streets were muddy quagmires, and a sharp line of uncut forest marked the ridgeline and the wilderness beyond. As industries grew, Duluth experienced boom cycles. Many architectural landmarks remain from these eras. Regal homes were built and tracks were laid for streetcars. The streetcars ran from Gary/New Duluth on the west end of the city to Lester Park on the east, stopping in the neighborhoods of Piedmont, Woodland and Park Point. An incline railroad built at Seventh Avenue West hauled passengers in trolley cars between Superior Street and Duluth Heights. Opera houses, hotels and railyards were sure signs of the prosperity that came to Duluth as a result of the booming natural resource-based economy of the late 1800s through the mid-1900s. The Twin Ports helped provide the lumber and iron ore to build the nation.

Many families came to work and finance this economic expansion. The names on schools, streets, parks, foundations and companies honor their investment in this community and help keep their stories alive.

Historical marker at Fond du Lac

Great Water Highway

Travel routes and commerce in the Great Lakes region were established long before the arrival of Europeans. Traders had summer rendezvous at the major portage sites and at intersections of the old canoe routes. Mackinac Island, Sault Ste. Marie, Madeline Island, Fort William, Grand Portage and Fond du Lac all had major trading posts. Furs would arrive from the interior in the late spring, and over a matter of weeks, business would be conducted until it was time to return to trapping areas while the lakes and rivers were still open and navigable.

This early trade required open water, free of ice, to move trade goods. Ice break-up, or iceout, is still an important seasonal event in this region, much for the same reason. The inland lakes experience iceout between the end of April and the first week of May. Lake Superior experiences the break-up over a period of weeks; the ice floes—large chunks of ice—shift around with the wind and water currents.

Lake Superior ice

Cutter *Sundew* breaking harbor ice

Spring thaw on an inland lake

As the St. Lawrence Seaway freezes up to ship traffic around January, the shipping season ends with the last foreign vessel leaving Duluth in December. However, boat traffic on the Great Lakes lasts into mid-January. While Lake Superior rarely freezes over entirely (once every 20 years), it does so frequently enough that ships look for winter berths from mid-January through mid-March. The U.S. Coast Guard in Duluth uses its local cutter and others from Thunder Bay and Sault Ste. Marie for icebreaking duties.

Portages

To travel between Lake Superior and its northern drainages, early explorers and traders used three main portage routes. These portages are located along the St. Louis River near Fond du Lac, at Grand Portage on the Pigeon River, and at Fort William (present-day Thunder Bay, Ontario) on the Kaministikwia River.

Portages are areas at which canoes and their cargoes have to be carried in order to bypass rapids or waterfalls, or to reach another section of navigable water. Major portages were natural places for camps, trading posts and communities to appear.

Canoeing inland lakes

Major portages were natural places for camps, trading posts and communities to appear.

Portage connecting inland lakes

Duluth Ship Canal

Excavation for the Duluth ship canal began in 1870 near the site of what was known as "Little Portage"—the narrowest part of Minnesota Point. Next to the ship canal, in front of the Army Corps of Engineers building, a plaque set in granite reads: "The nearby canal marks the site of Little Portage on Minnesota Point, crossed on June 27th, 1679 by Daniel Greysolon, Sieur du Lhut, a gentleman of the royal guard of Louis XIV on his way to explore the upper Mississippi."

As early speculators vied to increase commerce and build up Duluth, efforts were made to establish a railroad terminal and harbor facilities on the Duluth side of the harbor. In the late 1860s, Howard's Dock (also known as Citizens' Dock) was built, extending out into Lake Superior from a point close to Fifth Avenue East. But this structure could not be maintained due to the severity of winter storms, and was destroyed by the Lake.

Sunrise over the Duluth lift bridge and ship canal

<< **Aerial view of Duluth ship canal**

A saltie in the Duluth ship canal

It was determined that digging a canal through to safer moorings on St. Louis Bay was the only way to win any economic competition with neighboring Superior. A group of Duluth business investors formed a company that would build such a canal. Using the dredge *Ishpeming*, digging began in the summer of 1870. By the time winter arrived and the weather forced the operation to shut down, the canal was two-thirds of the way through.

Meanwhile, fears had mounted on the Superior side that the diversion of the St. Louis River's outflow through the new canal would negatively impact the natural outlet on Superior's side of the harbor. Superior city leaders appealed to various departments of the federal government, including the War Department, and a court injunction was awarded to halt the project.

On the evening of Friday, June 9th, 1871, Duluth mayor J.B. Culver received a telegram from the federal government with the injunction. It notified him that an army officer from Ft. Leavenworth would arrive by train to serve the papers. After checking the train schedules, it was determined the earliest the officer could arrive was Monday, June 12. Local legend has it that a group of 80 volunteers with picks and shovels worked alongside the *Ishpeming* day and night to finish digging through Minnesota Point before the officer arrived. By Sunday night, the St. Louis River was flowing out the channel. By Monday morning the force of water flowing out had widened the cut to 30 feet. The sides of the canal were eventually stabilized with timber and later with cement piers.

To answer Superior's protest, the city of Duluth put up a $100,000 bond to erect a dike in the harbor, which would prevent the St. Louis River from being diverted through the new canal. The dike was built, but after storms and mysterious circumstances, it was breached. By 1887, the federal government had taken over harbor operations, discovered the dike was unnecessary and removed what was left of it.

Boatwatchers lining the pier of the ship canal

Ship canal awash in November storm

Excavation for the ship canal began in 1870 near the site of what was known as "Little Portage"—the narrowest point across Minnesota Point.

The Aerial Lift Bridge

The plan to dredge a ship canal into Duluth's natural harbor required cutting through the narrowest part of Minnesota Point. Once the canal was complete, Minnesota Point had been turned into an island. This aggravated property owners on the newly-created island, as they found themselves suddenly disconnected from the mainland. A Mr. Wilhelm Boeing, in particular, tried several times to impede ship traffic with ropes.

Various means were tried to solve the problem of getting people on and off Minnesota Point. A fare-based rowboat ferry service was tried, but of course, this was only possible when the water was rowable. In early years during the winter, planks were laid on the ice with guide ropes attached to posts. Later, a rope suspension bridge was built during winter months. But it was flimsy and swayed violently in the wind. Park Pointers were threatening to secede to Superior if things didn't improve. By 1897, many summer homes were being built on the Point, and a steam ferry replaced the rowboat.

The "Duluth Aerial Ferry Bridge," designed by Thomas McGilvray, was completed in 1905. It was inspired by the Anodin Bridge in Rouen, France, the only other one like it in the world. Passengers could cross the canal on this early version of the bridge via a platform suspended on rails from the steel superstructure and pulled horizontally back and forth. It could hold up to 125,000 pounds. The early schedule was 12 trips an hour from 5 a.m. to midnight.

In 1929, it was modified to become the present "Aerial Lift Bridge" with the addition of a roadbed and counterweights. The clearance was raised to a height of 172 feet to better accommodate larger ships.

A ship entering the harbor will blast its horn in long-short patterns to signal its approach, or communicate by radio with the bridge tender. With a single push of a button, the bridge is raised to allow it to enter.

Laker passing under Lift Bridge

Spring arrives in the Duluth harbor

Sunset over the Lift Bridge and Park Point

Ship under the Lift Bridge

Excursion boat passes the Lift Bridge

Locals who are late because of waiting for the bridge to be lowered can be heard using this excuse: "I was bridged." It's a small price to pay for a symbol of personal identity for Duluth, its citizens and admirers.

Sailing Vessels

In the late 1600s, the common vessel used to move trade goods on the Great Lakes was the 36-foot Montreal canoe, manned by a dozen paddlers. Goods were shifted from the Montreals to smaller 24-foot birch bark canoes, which portaged and paddled across lakes and connecting routes all the way to Hudson Bay. In time, lightweight pine-plank bateaux and small sailboats called Mackinaws replaced the canoes.

Larger sailing vessels appeared on Lake Superior around 1770. These were schooners—wooden ships with two or more masts, typically with a capacity of 40 to 85 tons—that were built for the fur companies. By the early 1800s, the fur companies also became involved in commercial fishing enterprises and required even larger schooners.

Beginning in the 1850s, steamboats called on remote fishing villages along the North Shore. As more and more miners, fishermen and lumberjacks arrived in the rich and roadless wilderness in the 1880s, regular steamboat service was developed. All supplies were brought by boat, and in turn, boats transported all the fish, lumber and iron ore from the North Shore to market. Highway 61 was completed in 1926, which meant that goods could be transported along the North Shore by land as well as water.

Steel-hulled ships appeared on the Great Lakes in the 1880s. A unique design called the "whaleback" was first created and built in Duluth and Superior by Captain Alexander McDougall. The 600-foot "straight-deckers" began to appear by the early 1900s. These were the longest ships the Soo Locks connecting Lake Superior to the rest of the Great Lakes could accommodate at the time. But by 1972, with modifications to the Soo Locks, vessels reaching 1,000 feet long were sailing the Great Lakes.

Lake boat arriving while saltie lies anchored

A variety of modern watercraft on Lake Superior

Weather

Lake Superior's size dramatically influences the weather of the surrounding region. This means it is usually cooler by the Lake in summer and warmer by the Lake in winter. The average low temperatures occur in January around –2.2° F, and the average high temperatures are usually in July around 77° F. Duluth's average annual rainfall is 30 inches. Lake effect snow can be significant, particularly for communities on the South Shore. The average annual snowfall in Duluth is 78 inches. Notorious seasonal storms can produce waves over 20 feet high. Lake Superior is the final resting place for more than 350 shipwrecks, including the Columbia Steamship vessel *Edmund Fitzgerald*.

The Northern Lights provide a spectacular light show on a clear night. They can occur year-round, but are noticed more frequently on long winter nights.

Ice at the grain docks

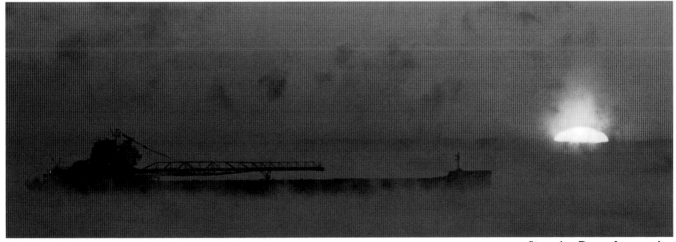

Steaming December sunrise

Aurora borealis—the Northern Lights

Lake Superior is the final resting place for more than 350 shipwrecks, including the Columbia Steamship vessel Edmund Fitzgerald.

November storm

Early winter steam in the harbor

Ice in Superior Port entry

Shipwrecks

Since shipping began on Lake Superior in 1835, more than 350 ships have been lost. Twenty-four have simply disappeared, leaving no trace of wreckage. Only one Montreal canoe—one of the earliest vessels for transporting goods—was known to be lost. As ships made the transition from sail to steam and eventually from wood to steel, navigational and forecasting technology had trouble keeping up. Captains felt the economic pressure to haul as many cargoes as possible in a season. Pushing the limits of ship and weather likely played a part in the losses.

Raging storms during the last week of November in 1905 claimed 78 lives and disabled or destroyed 29 ships on Lake Superior. The *Mataafa* was blown perpendicular across the Duluth Ship Canal piers during the great storm of November 29, 1905. It beached and began to break up, but rescue was impossible due to the storm. Nine of her crewmembers perished in view of Duluth.

November storms are notorious. "The Gales of November" is a phrase made familiar by the song, "The Wreck of the *Edmund Fitzgerald*," composed by Gordon Lightfoot to memorialize the sinking of the *Fitzgerald* just off Whitefish Point, Michigan, on November 10, 1975. All 29 members of the crew died. With improved weather forecasting technology and lifesaving equipment, such major calamities are now rare. Ships still occasionally run aground. In November of 1985, the ocean-going ship *Socrates* was blown onto Park Point during a storm. The *Fraser* ran aground during a heavy fog in August of 2002.

Many ships were salvaged and returned to service after mishaps on the Lake. But the *Thomas Wilson*, a whaleback steamer that sank just off the Duluth Ship Canal after being struck in broad daylight by the *George G. Hadley* on June 7, 1902, is still on the bottom of the Lake. The 308-foot vessel and nine of the 20 crewmembers were lost within three minutes of the collision. The *Thomas Wilson*, badly damaged and heavily loaded with iron ore, was too difficult to bring to the surface at that time.

Wreck of the *S.S. Ontario* on Battle Island

Of the more than 350 ships that have been lost since Lake Superior shipping began in 1835, twenty-four have simply disappeared, leaving no trace of wreckage.

Lighthouses

The lighthouses at Whitefish Point and Copper Harbor, Michigan, built in 1848, were the first on the shores of Lake Superior. They were two of 76 raised on the Great Lakes in a building phase that lasted until 1852. Most lighthouses marked harbors and river entrances, others marked shoals, reefs, islands and points. At that time, lighthouses burned whale oil and used reflectors to magnify the light. Lightkeepers tended the wicks in all weather. With the overhaul of the U.S. Lighthouse system, which came underway in about 1850, a group of qualified inspectors was put in place along with the gradual adoption of new technology, which included the Fresnel Lens. These lenses were comprised of smaller lenses and glass prisms configured in a beehive shape to magnify and direct the light into a single beam, or plane, visible at great distances.

Ship traffic on the Great Lakes grew quickly. In 1888, Chicago had 20,000 ship arrivals and departures, compared to New York's 23,000. In that same year, 8,832 ships passed through the Soo Locks. By 1910, there were 334 major lighted navigational aids, 67 fog signals and 563 buoys on the Great Lakes.

The Minnesota Point Lighthouse is the oldest standing structure in Duluth. In 1823 Lt. Henry Woolsey Bayfield of the

Minnesota Point lighthouse

South pier lighthouse

Moonrise over the Duluth entry lighthouses

The innermost harbor lighthouse was placed on the canal's south breakwater in 1873 and replaced with the current structure in 1901.

Inner harbor lighthouse

British Royal Navy identified this location as the "zero point" for lake charts. The lighthouse was commissioned by U.S. Congress in 1855 and construction was completed in 1858. It was decommissioned in 1878. It is located past the current Sky Harbor Airport near the present Superior Port entry.

Duluth Port Entry Lights

The innermost harbor lighthouse was placed on the canal's south pier in 1873 and replaced with the current structure in 1901. The original outer light on the south pier was built in 1889 and replaced in 1901 to work in tandem with the inner light as range lights. The north pier light was built as a result of a 1908 report describing the approach to the Duluth Harbor as one of the most dangerous on the Great Lakes because only the south pier was lit. The north pier light was put in service in April of 1910 with a Fifth-Order Fresnel Lens.

Storm passing by north pier light

The North Shore

Split Rock Lighthouse

In the early twentieth century, ship crews recognized the waters along the North Shore as some of the most treacherous to navigate. Extremely deep water lured ships too close to shore, and iron ore deposits caused compass readings to fluctuate dangerously. Split Rock Lighthouse was built in 1910 in answer to the needs of the increasing ship traffic (and increasing wrecks) on Lake Superior. Equipped with a Third-Order Fresnel Lens, the official range of its beam was 22 miles. This lighthouse is located on a dramatic rock bluff overlooking the shoreline 124 feet below. At the time it was built, the lighthouse could be reached only by boat. Building materials and supplies were hoisted up the cliff from the shore. It is the most photographed lighthouse on Lake Superior, and one of the most visited lighthouses in the country. The site includes the lighthouse, fog signal house, oil storage building, three barns, three lightkeepers' houses and a museum operated by the Minnesota Historical Society. Once a year on November 10th, Split Rock Lighthouse is lit to commemorate the sinking of the *Edmund Fitzgerald*. It is about 45 miles northeast of Duluth.

Two Harbors Lighthouse

Two Harbors Lighthouse

The Two Harbors Light Station was completed in 1892 and is now the oldest operating light station on the North Shore. Built to guide ships into the iron ore docks on Agate Bay, this red-brick, two-story structure combines the lighthouse and its keeper's house. The tower stands 49 feet tall. Its original Fourth-Order Fresnel Lens was replaced in 1970 with rotating electric beacons. The keeper's house is now a bed & breakfast. The gift shop and self-guided tours are open to the public to explore the original lighthouse, fog signal house and the oil house, and to see up close the ship activity along the North Shore. Two Harbors is about 30 miles northeast of Duluth.

Ore docks at Two Harbors

Ore Docks at Two Harbors

Great views of Two Harbors' Agate Bay ore docks can be seen from the parking lot next to the lighthouse and public boat launch. Dock #1 (closest to the shore) was once the largest ore dock in the world. In 1883, the Duluth & Iron Range Railway began construction to connect Agate Bay with iron mines in Tower, Minnesota, 70 miles away. It took 600 men from June to December that year to build the first 20 miles, overcoming swamps, rocky ridges, ravines and rivers.

Gooseberry Falls State Park

The Gooseberry River began appearing on explorers' maps as early as 1670. Before North Shore tourism became popular around the 1920s, the area around the Falls was used for commercial and recreational fishing, as well as logging. The Gooseberry Falls area was authorized for preservation in 1933. The Civilian Conservation Corps (CCC) set up camp and built the park's stone and log buildings, campgrounds, trails and picnic areas. The true centerpiece of the park is a series of gorgeous waterfalls that rush through eroded basalt lava flows out into Lake Superior. This is a haven for rock hounds, as the mouth of the river is a great place to comb the beach for agates. Gooseberry Falls State Park is about 40 miles from Duluth.

Gooseberry Falls

Commercial Fishing

A true commercial fishing industry has always struggled to survive on Lake Superior. As large as the Lake is, it is simply too cold to support the nutrient levels needed for large populations of fish to grow and reproduce quickly enough to sustain intense harvesting. In addition, the introduction of the parasitic sea lamprey helped decimate Lake Superior's large fish stock until this invasive species came under control.

As the fur trade began to decline in 1835 and finally bottomed out in 1840, the American Fur Company attempted to remain viable by turning to Lake Superior's fish resource. Their success was limited, with only a handful of schooners plying the waters for lake trout and whitefish. To encourage settlement along the North Shore, the territorial leadership promoted the area primarily to Scandinavian immigrants for its commercial fishing opportunities. It wasn't until 1870, when the railroad finally linked Duluth to the Twin Cities of Minneapolis and St. Paul, that commercial fishing became truly feasible. This reliable method of transportation allowed the fish to be sold and shipped quickly to large markets.

Commercial fishing sign

Thirty-two species of fish are native to Lake Superior. Initially, the large whitefish, lake trout and bluefin were harvested. By 1908, the most common fish harvested was the smaller herring.

The fishing industry dwindled by the mid 1900s, though today there are still a few commercial fishing companies in the Twin Ports and some scattered along the North Shore. Recreational charter fishing is very popular, and even if you don't catch your own, fresh and smoked fish can be purchased in villages along the North Shore.

Old commercial fishing camp on the North Shore

Ship Building

Resting soundly on Superior's waterfront is a truly unique vessel, the *S.S. Meteor*. Often mistaken for a submarine, this was one of 42 whalebacks built in the Twin Ports between 1888 and 1898 under the direction of Captain Alexander McDougall. Whalebacks were the first steel-hulled ships to carry iron ore and grain from the head of the Lakes. The *Meteor* is the last of its kind.

Fraser Shipyards

McDougall, a Scottish immigrant, became one of the youngest captains to sail the Great Lakes. He envisioned a ship that would be economical to build, maximize carrying capacity and outsmart—so to speak—the rough waves of the inland seas.

McDougall's whaleback ship design featured a rounded hull and a rounded upper deck designed to shed water. The whalebacks had a mere 8-foot deck clearance above the water, which allowed them to ride through the waves instead of over them. To sailors, they were known as "pigboats," because their rounded bows resembled a pig's snout.

McDougall had difficulty finding financing for his unusual design in New York, so he organized his own company and attempted to buy land for a shipyard on Duluth's waterfront. When he was unable to meet the price for land in Duluth, the city of Superior offered him land and cash to build on the site that is now Fraser Shipyards. McDougall partnered with Julius Barnes during World War I to build another shipyard in Riverside (West Duluth), which constructed 46 small ocean-going vessels.

The whaleback *S.S. Meteor* on display at Barker's Island in Superior, WI.

During World War II there were eight shipyards in the Twin Ports. Combined, they built 230 watercraft between 1941 and 1944. Shipbuilding dwindled after this time, and Fraser Shipyards of Superior is the last shipbuilder in the Twin Ports. It still has two dry-docks to build and service boats and ships.

Iron Ore

In the mid-1800s, rumors of copper, silver and gold in northeastern Minnesota lured investors from the East Coast. When the treaties between the federal government and Native American groups were completed in 1854, prospectors and speculators moved into the area around Lake Superior. While the copper, silver and gold never amounted to much, the iron ore in the Arrowhead Region of Minnesota proved to be a source of incredible wealth.

Iron ore deposits were noted in the early 1700s by French explorers, but it wasn't until the systematic surveys of the 1840s and 1850s that a rough picture of Minnesota's iron ore deposits emerged. Three main ranges that would come to be known as the Mesabi, Cuyuna and Vermilion developed in northeastern Minnesota and used Duluth as their major port.

Operating 24 hours a day, a laker loads ore at night

The discovery of iron ore started a chain of events that was very important for Duluth. As the demand for iron ore grew, new mines opened on each of the ranges. Additional workers arrived to take jobs at the mines, and towns grew in response. Because more ore was being mined, better ways of transporting it had to be established, and railroads were built or expanded to move the ore. Railroad jobs brought another wave of people. More ore at the Duluth docks meant an increase in ship traffic, which necessitated more docks, bigger ships and more workers. All this activity brought undreamed-of wealth to the area.

Between 1890 and 1900, Minnesota's ore ranges produced 43,000,000 tons. In the next decade, production grew to 208,600,000 tons. Output increased again during war years, then dropped off. The Vermilion Range produced until 1963, and the last Cuyuna ore was shipped in 1977. Of the three ranges, the Mesabi is the only one still producing ore.

Taconite and limestone waiting to be loaded

During the height of Minnesota's iron ore production, a few industrial giants began to consolidate smaller companies. Eventually United States Steel controlled most of Minnesota's iron range and the railroads that moved the ore.

Railroading

Railroading was booming in the 1800s, and the Twin Ports of Duluth and Superior were fertile grounds for entrepreneurs of all stripes. But the two railroad barons who made the biggest impact were Jay Cooke and James J. Hill.

Railroading was an expensive and risky venture. Only the federal government could supply the land grants and loans needed to push the rails through expanses of unsettled territory, but since railroads were the only reliable transportation to these areas, the risk was deemed worth taking.

In 1868 Jay Cooke, Abraham Lincoln's financier for the Northern Army of the Civil War, arrived in Duluth to evaluate the area for possible railroad investors. The level ground of Superior was already platted, bought and sold. However, land was available for sale in Duluth. After forming the Western Land Association, he promptly bought up most of the commercial property in Duluth.

Jay Cooke

Fueled by the desire to develop a port to rival Chicago's, Cooke wanted to connect Duluth to St. Paul with the Lake Superior & Mississippi Railroad south through Cloquet, bypassing Superior. He also wanted a transcontinental railroad—the Northern Pacific Railroad—to connect Lake Superior to the Pacific Ocean. Between his involvement in the group dredging the Duluth Ship Canal and the construction of the Northern Pacific Railroad over the rocky ridge of Duluth, Cooke's firm (the federal agent of railroad financing) became overextended and failed. Though Cooke's railroads were eventually completed, this failure was blamed for triggering the domino effect of the nationwide financial panic of 1873. In two months, the population of Duluth dropped from over 5,000 to 1,300 people. More than half the businesses in Duluth closed.

In 1883 James J. Hill, the biggest railroad baron of the Midwest, swooped into the Twin Ports and bought up property in Superior. Hill had a practice of building railroads for the long-term. He looked for the most geologically level, and thus

DM&IR train heads to the Iron Range with limestone

the most economically feasible routes to build and operate railroads. This led him to building the Eastern Railway of Minnesota between Superior and St. Paul. The original right-of-way is still used by Burlington Northern/Santa Fe.

At one time 50 passenger trains a day arrived at and departed from the Duluth Union Depot. Passenger service ended in the early 1980s. Railroading in the Twin Ports has seen many start-ups and mergers since the late 1880s, and consolidations continue to occur. Currently, the railroads haul grain and coal from western states, and taconite pellets (reduced iron ore) from the Iron Range of northeastern Minnesota.

In the beginning of the 1900s, Duluth was the leading lumber producer in the U.S. Around 1920, approximately 350 miles of temporary tracks connected North Shore docks to the great pine stands north of Lake Superior.

Gradually, the old railroad yards around Garfield Avenue were taken over by I-35 and development by the light industry. The remaining Garfield Avenue tracks are used by Burlington Northern/Santa Fe as a sorting yard. Their main yards are now in Superior.

The first locomotive in Minnesota, the *William Crooks*, can be seen at the Depot, formally known as the St. Louis County Heritage & Arts Center.

North Shore Scenic Railroad

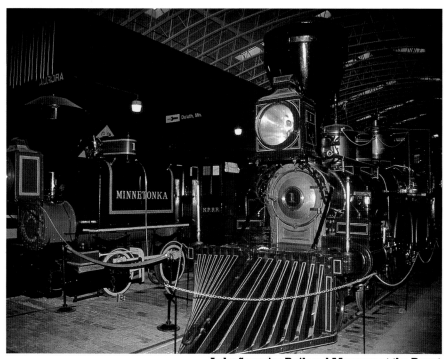

Lake Superior Railroad Museum at the Depot

Currently, the railroads haul grain and coal from western states, and taconite pellets (reduced iron ore) from the Iron Range of northeastern Minnesota.

Lumber

The first sawmill in the area—equipped with a two-man whipsaw—began operation in Fond du Lac around 1840. Many of these early types of sawmills were set up to serve the region's immediate need to build housing for the numerous settlers arriving in the area. Around 1870, the Lake Superior & Mississippi Railroad from St. Paul to Duluth was complete, and Duluth experienced an increase in economic development as a result. The demand for lumber grew, and so did the sawmills.

Logs from the Arrowhead Region were transported on temporary logging railroads to the shore of Lake Superior. From there, the logs were floated, boomed and towed to Duluth for milling. In the mid-1880s, totals were reaching 10 million feet of lumber cut per year, of which almost all was white pine. The peak year for cutting was in 1911, when 244 million board feet went through the mills. The decline was as dramatic as the increase; in 1921, only 11 million board feet were cut.

Today the old growth forests have been cut, except for rare small stands of white pines. Modern logging is on reforested stands of timber or on plantations. A variety of local companies still process timber for pulpwood, paper mills and lumber.

Mill bound logs

Unloading logs at a Duluth paper mill

<< **Minnesota's forests are rich**

Modern Shipping

Two important seasonal events in Duluth are the shipping season opener in mid-March, and the shipping season closing in mid-January. These are marked by the first ocean vessel entering the port in the spring, and the last one leaving in December with its holds full of grain, and the first and last of the lake boat traffic.

Two general types of vessels call on the Twin Ports. Salties are ocean-going ships, usually with foreign registries. They have pointed bows, derricks (cranes) mounted on their decks, and generally carry in a load such as lumber and take out a load of grain (wheat or soybeans).

The most common vessels are the huge lake boats or lakers. They travel only on fresh water and are 600–1,000 feet long with either pointed or rounded bows. Some may have a self-unloader mounted on the deck, others are simple straight-deckers. Lake boats are registered either in Canada or the U.S. and haul iron ore, coal, cement, limestone and grain.

As the load capacity of ships has increased, the number of ships and voyage frequency have decreased. Still, huge crowds of boatwatchers gather along the Duluth Ship Canal and at the Lake Superior Maritime Visitor Center, watching the ships pass under the Aerial Lift Bridge.

Cargoes that require special handling from ship to rail can be accommodated. Cargo terminals consist of multi-purpose bulk terminals, a cargo distribution center, ore docks, a coal dock and grain elevators with a capacity of 55 million bushels.

The Duluth port is ranked No. 1 nationally for iron ore and No. 5 for coal. On the U.S. Great Lakes it ranks No. 1 for grain. Total cargo volume for the port is ranked No. 1 on the Great Lakes, and No. 21 nationally.

Seaway locks can accommodate ocean-going ships up to 730 feet long. The locks at Sault Ste. Marie can handle lake boats up to 1,000 feet long, 105 feet wide and with a draft (the depth of

Port of Duluth can handle specialized cargo

Foreign freighter taking on grain

the keel below the water line) of 27 feet. The locks help ships overcome the 20-foot drop from Lake Superior into Lake Huron by raising and lowering them as they pass through the St. Marys River.

Passenger vessels can be seen on rare occasions. Most have foreign registries. One or two U.S. companies are working on the logistics of scheduling cruises on the Great Lakes. It is one of the most dreamed-of excursions for many visitors to the Great Lakes region.

Foreign freighter taking on cargo

Port of Duluth's main bulk cargo terminals

German cruise ship making a rare port of call

Cargo terminals consist of multi-purpose bulk terminals, a cargo distribution center, ore docks, a coal dock and grain elevators with a capacity of 55 million bushels.

USAF
MINNESOTA
DULUTH INT'L.
AIRPORT
Dedicated To Those Who Serve

Aviation

Land for Duluth International Airport was purchased from St. Louis County in 1929 and originally had two 2,650-foot sod runways. After World War II, the U.S. Air Force and the Minnesota Air National Guard (MNANG) constructed facilities at the east end of the field. MNANG continues its operations, though the Air Force operations have ceased. Over the years, runways were added and extended, and a new terminal building was completed in 1974.

In 1994, Cirrus Design, a company that designs and builds personal aircraft, outgrew its original facilities and relocated to Duluth. It employs more than 850 workers, and its personal aircraft are industry leaders in performance and safety.

Northwest Airlines keeps a maintenance and inspection base at Duluth for A-320 Airbuses, DC-9s, Boeing 757s and others.

Recalling a simpler and a more rugged aviation era, Sky Harbor Airport on Minnesota Point handles numerous floatplanes and offers rides during the summer months.

Sky Harbor Airport on Minnesota Point

Education

Many students have found a home in the Twin Ports as they study and learn at Duluth and Superior's excellent institutions. Duluth is home to the University of Minnesota Duluth (UMD) and the College of St. Scholastica (CSS). Superior is the home of the University of Wisconsin Superior (UWS). Both cities also have technical schools and community colleges.

University of Minnesota Duluth

UMD is a comprehensive regional university that offers 12 bachelor's degrees in 75 majors, 19 graduate programs including a two-year program at the School of Medicine, and a four-year College of Pharmacy program. UMD's total enrollment is over 10,000 students, and it employs over 1,700 faculty and staff members. Located on a 244-acre campus overlooking Lake Superior, most of the buildings are connected by hallways and concourses, giving students an option to stay inside when the weather is less than favorable.

University of Minnesota Duluth

UMD Library

Enrollment increases have led to new construction of dorms, a library, science buildings and the Weber Music Hall. UMD is also home to the Natural Resource Research Institute. In 1895, the state legislature created the Normal School of Duluth, which evolved into the Duluth State Teachers College in 1921. In 1947 it became an affiliate campus of the University of Minnesota.

College of St. Scholastica

CSS is an independent private college. It was founded in 1912 by a pioneering group of Benedictine Sisters as a college for women. Today it educates both men and women, offering undergraduate and graduate degrees with an emphasis on behavioral and health sciences. It is located on 186 acres, also with a spectacular view of Lake Superior. Total enrollment reaches over 2,800 with a student-to-faculty ratio of 13:1.

University of Wisconsin Superior

UWS is a comprehensive public university in the University of Wisconsin system. Founded in 1893, the Superior Normal School was first established to train teachers in the latest in classroom methods. These newly educated teachers were in high demand in the small towns and rural districts of northern Wisconsin, Minnesota and Michigan. Today, the school offers over 30 undergraduate and graduate degrees. It has a total enrollment of 2,800 with a 17:1 student-to-faculty ratio.

UMD Bulldogs hockey at the DECC

University of Wisconsin Superior

Many students have found a home in the Twin Ports as they study and learn at Duluth and Superior's excellent institutions.

Regional Medical Center

Duluth's medical community serves northern Minnesota, Wisconsin and Michigan's Upper Peninsula. In addition to the contributions this community makes to the health of the region, it also provides more than 8,000 jobs.

St. Luke's

St. Luke's, Duluth's first hospital, was founded by St. Paul's Episcopal Church in 1881 when typhoid fever had reached epidemic levels in the city. The health care clinic that had its roots in a small room above a blacksmith's shop has grown to a multi-specialty hospital with over 2,000 employees, as well as a regional health care system of 25 primary and specialty clinics. St. Luke's prides itself on having kept an important value through over a century of expansion: the patient comes first.

St. Luke's Hospital

St. Mary's/Duluth Clinic and the Miller-Dwan Medical Center

St. Mary's/Duluth Clinic (SMDC) is a multi-specialty hospital with over 5,500 employees. St. Mary's was founded in 1888 by a small group of Benedictine sisters, when Duluth's population was about 33,000. With more immigrants and lumberjacks in the region, the sisters sold "lumberjack tickets" to keep the hospital afloat and raise money for better facilities. The tickets sold for about $1–$5 per year and entitled purchasers to medical care at St. Mary's—much like an insurance plan.

Five physicians organized the Duluth Clinic in 1915. As Duluth expanded, more physicians came on board and facilities were enlarged to meet the growing medical needs of the community. The Duluth Clinic merged with St. Mary's in the late 1990s and is the state's third largest multi-specialty group practice. SMDC provides a huge array of complementary services.

The Miller-Dwan Medical Center was built primarily with the generous donations from Andreas Miller in 1917 and Mary Dwan in 1971. It was a public hospital until 1990, when it became a freestanding, nonprofit hospital. It merged with SMDC in 2001.

Miller-Dwan Medical Center

Architectural
Landmarks

Old Duluth Central High School

When the Old Duluth Central High School was completed in 1892, Secretary of the Interior John W. Noble remarked at its opening: "Your new high school is the finest building of its kind I ever saw. There is no public school building equal to it in the United States."

Old Central is a wonderful example of Romanesque architecture. Built by two Duluthian architects, Palmer & Hall, it was completed at a cost of approximately $460,000, including the clock tower. The clock was imported from Paris, and the chimes were designed to sound like those of Westminster in London. Materials also included brownstone quarried near Fond du Lac. With architecture so beautiful and classic, it was used as the backdrop for the city of Winnipeg in the movie *Iron Will*.

Old Duluth Central High School is located at Lake Avenue and Second Street. It is now the Central Administration Building for the Duluth Public Schools. In addition to housing the district's administrative offices, it also offers special educational programs for the district.

The Depot/St. Louis County Heritage & Arts Center

One way to get to know Duluth on many levels is to explore the St. Louis County Heritage & Arts Center, otherwise known as the Depot. In 1892 this Union Railroad Depot was built by the Boston firm of Peabody, Stearns & Furber, in the beautiful French Norman architectural style. By 1910, trains from seven different rail lines were arriving at and departing from the Union Depot, with up to 5,000 passengers daily. It was placed on the National Register of Historic Places in 1971. After major renovations, the Union Depot reopened in 1973 as an area cultural center. The historic part of the building features exhibits by four different museums. The west wing houses the Duluth Playhouse and administrative offices.

The Depot

Glensheen

The Depot is home to the Duluth Art Institute, the Duluth Children's Museum, the St. Louis County Historical Society Museum, the Lake Superior Railroad Museum and Veteran's Memorial Hall. The North Shore Scenic Railroad operates from the Depot.

Glensheen

At one time, Duluth boasted more millionaires per capita than anywhere in the country. A variety of architectural designs can be seen in the eastern neighborhoods and along London Road. Glensheen, which resembles an early seventeenth-century English country estate, was built in 1905–1908 on 7.6 acres for the Chester A. Congdon family. In 1968, the heirs of Chester and Clara Congdon donated Glensheen to the University of Minnesota. On July 28, 1979, the estate was opened to the public as a museum. Since then, over 2 million people have experienced a visit to Glensheen. The majority of the furnishings are original to the date the family moved in, including the children's clothing in their closets. The grounds burst with color as the formal gardens bloom in the spring and summer. It is one of the many stately homes that can be seen along London Road, from 26th Avenue East to the Lester River at 60th Avenue East.

Fitger's

August Fitger was a young German immigrant who graduated from one of Germany's premier brewing schools as a brewmaster. He was hired in 1881 by Michael Fink, owner of Fink's Lake Superior Brewery. By 1882, Fitger owned half the brewery.

In 1884 he acquired a partner, Percy Anneke, and the brewery was renamed the A. Fitger & Co./Lake Superior Brewery. During Prohibition, the brewery continued to stay active

Fitger's Brewery Complex on the Lakewalk

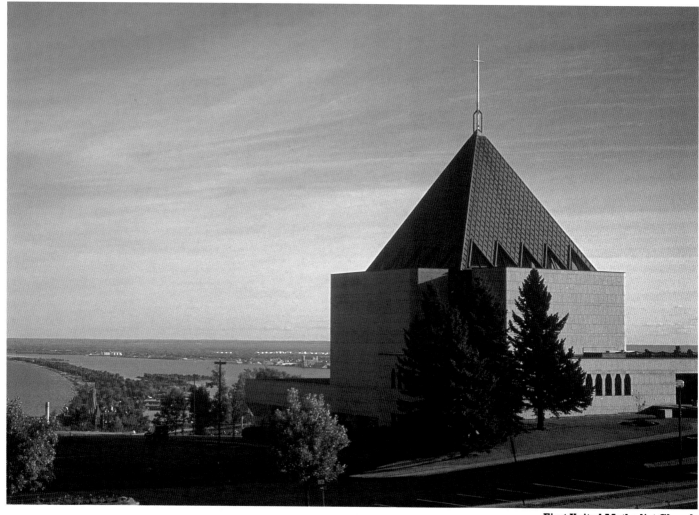

First United Methodist Church

by bottling soda pop and making candy bars. After the repeal, Fitger's resumed brewing. Despite the national pattern, business boomed the 1930s.

In 1944, the Beerhalter family took over the business and continued to produce until 1972, when Fitger's closed. It was the end of 115 years in the business. Twelve years later, the Fitger's Brewery Complex re-opened. It has been extensively renovated and is now home to an historic inn, restaurants and shopping. Listed on the National Register of Historic Places, its location offers stunning views of the waterfront and Lakewalk.

First United Methodist Church

Commonly referred to as the Copper Top Church, it is a recognizable feature of the Duluth Skyline. Pietro Belluschi, Dean of Architecture and Planning at MIT in Boston, was the architect on the project. His vision—a place of worship that was modern, yet reminiscent of an ancient pyramid—was complete in 1966.

Duluth Public Library

Duluth Public Library

The architectural firm of Gunnar Birkerts & Associates (Bloomfield Hills, MI) was selected as the building architect in December 1968. The City bought the site for the Main Library in 1969. The Library opened for business on November 17, 1980. The Duluth Public Library hosts ongoing programs and classes, as well as book clubs, storytime groups and the annual used book sale.

Kitchi Gammi Club

The Kitchi Gammi Club is one of four buildings in Duluth with a neo-Gothic influence, designed by Bertram Goodhue from New York City. The Club was first designed as a private social club for businessmen in 1912, but today women are allowed as members. Located on East Superior Street south of St. Luke's Hospital, its classic old world flavor reminds us of the entrepreneurial spirit of Duluth.

Kitchi Gammi Club

Henry H. Meyers House

Located on East First Street this home was designed by Duluth architects Bray & Nystrom in a Romanesque style in 1910. The stone was excavated from a construction site just north of Superior St. at 24th Avenue E.

Arthur P. Cook House

Located on West Skyline Parkway, this home is a classic example of how the materials, design and location complement each other to make this a landmark on the Skyline. Duluth architect I. Vernon Hill designed it in 1900 for Mr. Cook, a visionary druggist and realtor.

Observation Hill

This home located on Observation Hill overlooking the railyards demonstrates how the topography of Duluth has influenced home design. Many homes on the Duluth hillside are built directly on bedrock.

Arthur P. Cook house

Observation Hill house built on bedrock

Diverse Community

The diversity of Duluth's cultural makeup had early starts. Beginning in the 1850s, immigrants were recruited to the Twin Ports and North Shore in an effort to build up the area's infrastructure. These early immigrants were mostly from Scandinavian countries, and were attracted to the area by the prospect of commercial fishing opportunities. A second wave of immigrants came around 1869 to build the Lake Superior & Mississippi Railroad. Recruiter advertisements from the era listed job openings for 3,000 railroad laborers and 10,000 settlers to buy land and settle along the rail lines. A major enticement was free transportation on the railroads for those settling on railroad land. By 1870, Duluth's population of about 3,000 was nearly 60% immigrants. Of these, half were from Scandinavian countries. The remaining half was comprised mainly of people from Ireland, Germany and Canada. These immigrant groups formed strong social and religious communities. The churches built by these groups are some of Duluth's most obvious signs of the thriving diversity present today. Duluth's rich heritage, beginning with the first Native American groups in the area, continues to grow today as people from around the globe settle here. Restaurants, bakeries, shops, music and art make for a wide variety of experiences.

Twelve Holy Apostles Greek Orthodox Church

St. Paul's Episcopal Church

St. Mark African Methodist Episcopal Church

Public Sculpture

Around 1990, downtown Duluth underwent an extensive redesign. One important objective of the renovation was to make the waterfront a focal point accessible to the public. Creating a visual representation of how the arts are valued by the community was another objective. The project incorporated commissioned pieces of sculpture, as well as classic reproductions and older works that were already present. Many pieces memorialize events and people from Duluth's history. Duluth's sculpture gardens are home to works from its sister cities in Canada, Sweden, Russia and Japan.

Spirit of Lake Superior **in Canal Park**

Leif Erickson

Fountain of the Wind **in Canal Park**

<< *Man, Child & Gull* **in Canal Park**

Attractions

Lake Superior Zoo

The Lake Superior Zoo in western Duluth is home to animals from all over the world. It had a simple beginning when Bert Onsgard, a Duluth businessman, constructed a pen for his pet deer. As the diversity and number of animals increased, so did the facilities. Today, one of the centerpieces of the zoo is the polar exhibit with Bubba and Berlin, its two polar bears. Eleven endangered species including the Snow Leopard, White-naped Crane and American Desert Tortoise are at home at the Lake Superior Zoo. Peregrine Falcons, Fennec Foxes and seventeen other threatened species also call the zoo home.

Lake Superior Maritime Visitor Center

The Lake Superior Maritime Visitor Center (previously called the Canal Park Maritime Museum) is located on the Duluth Ship Canal at the foot of the Aerial Lift Bridge. Maintained and operated by the U.S. Army Corps of Engineers, this free museum is one of the most visited in Minnesota. Displays describe the current ship traffic as well as interpret the maritime history, technology and shipwrecks of the past. A daily schedule of arriving and departing ship traffic is updated on monitors. You can also call the "Boatwatcher's Hotline" for estimated arrivals and departures. Watching a boat come in is fun for the whole family. You won't want to miss this classic picture-taking opportunity; it's all bells, whistles and horns as the ships signal for passage under the lift bridge.

Lake Superior Zoo

Lake Superior Maritime Visitor Center

S.S. William A. Irvin and *Lake Superior* tug

S.S. *William A. Irvin* Ore Boat Museum and the *Lake Superior* Tugboat

Now a floating museum, the *William A. Irvin* was the flagship of U.S. Steel's Great Lakes Fleet. The *Irvin* entered service in 1938 and carried ore on the Great Lakes for the next forty years. In addition, she hosted a variety of dignitaries and guests. The *Irvin* is a rare and remarkable combination of hardworking ore freighter and elegant ship, now permanently docked along the Duluth waterfront. She is open for tours during the summer months. Included in the tours is a visit to the *Lake Superior*, the historical Army Corps of Engineers tugboat.

Vista Fleet

The best way to get a firsthand, up-close view of the ship and dock activities of the Twin Ports harbor is to take a tour aboard a Vista Fleet vessel. They offer numerous tours of the Duluth/Superior harbor daily during the spring, summer and fall seasons. If weather permits, part of the fully narrated sightseeing tour is a trip under the Aerial Lift Bridge and out into Lake Superior. A special treat is the evening dinner-cruise.

Great Lakes Aquarium

The Great Lakes Aquarium (GLA) was created to build awareness for the precious resource of freshwater. A variety of aquariums house freshwater otters, ducks, turtles and fish like sturgeon, lake trout and herring. The GLA's touching tank is a popular stop where it's possible to handle freshwater creatures. Visitors of all ages enjoy the numerous hands-on

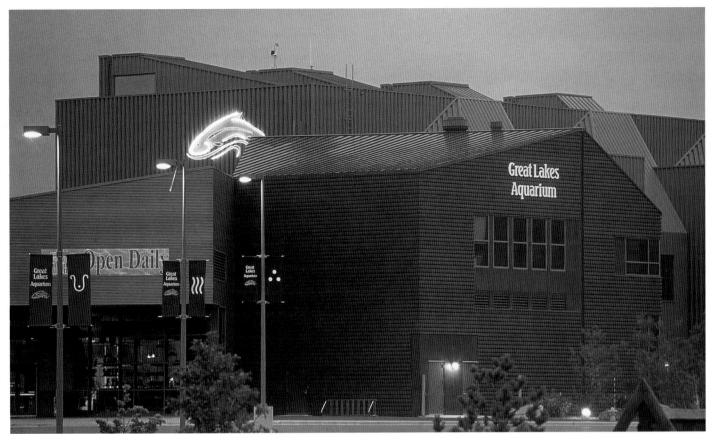

Great Lakes Aquarium

exhibits. Try piloting a virtual ore boat through the Duluth Ship Canal, or see how altering the shoreline creates different types of waves.

U.S. Coast Guard Cutter *Sundew*

Decommissioned in May of 2004, the *Sundew* is now a floating museum on Duluth's waterfront. The *Sundew* is 180 feet long. She was built right here in the Twin Ports in 1944 and is now docked near the *S.S. William A. Irvin*.

Retired U.S. Coast Guard cutter *Sundew*

Lake Superior Railroad Museum and the North Shore Scenic Railroad

Both these entities are housed at the Depot. During the tourist season, a variety of trips are scheduled daily on the North Shore Scenic Railroad. The Lake Superior Railroad Museum maintains a large collection of vintage equipment that fills seven tracks of the original platforms of the Union Depot. This visit is truly a step back in time.

Lake Superior Railroad Museum at The Depot

Canal Park

Duluth's waterfront has experienced a renaissance since 1990 with major downtown streetscape renovation and the extension of Interstate 35 to 26th Avenue East. A great deal of debate, discussion and planning took place to preserve and enhance the natural and historical attributes of the downtown area. Until that time the Canal Park neighborhood was still home to warehouses and light industrial business mixed in with a few bars and taverns. Now it has transformed into a fun, romantic shopping area used year-round by locals and visitors alike. *Outside Magazine* has rated Duluth as a Top Ten Dream Town.

Carriage rides in Canal Park

Canal Park, South Lake Avenue

Downtown Lakewalk

The Lakewalk stretches 4.2 miles along Lake Superior from 26th Avenue East to the Ship Canal and Bayfront Festival Park. The Lakewalk features a boardwalk and an adjacent paved trail for bikers, runners and inline skaters. Never far from Lake Superior, the Lakewalk offers excellent views of the waterfront. Along the eastern portion are the Duluth Rose Garden and Leif Erickson Park. At the western end is the Canal Park entertainment district and the Aerial Lift Bridge. Various types of public art and historical markers dot the route. Locals use it year-round and enjoy the exercise as well as the views of the Lake. It is a community focal point.

Bayfront Festival Park

What a gift! Thanks to a generous donation by Lois Paulucci, the Bayfront Festival Park has come to fruition. Home to outdoor concerts, festivals and skating parties, the park is a spectacular venue for outdoor celebrations for the entire family. One of the most widely known annual festivals held here is the Bayfront Blues Fest.

Concert at Bayfront Festival Park

Lakewalk as it passes between Fitger's and the Lake

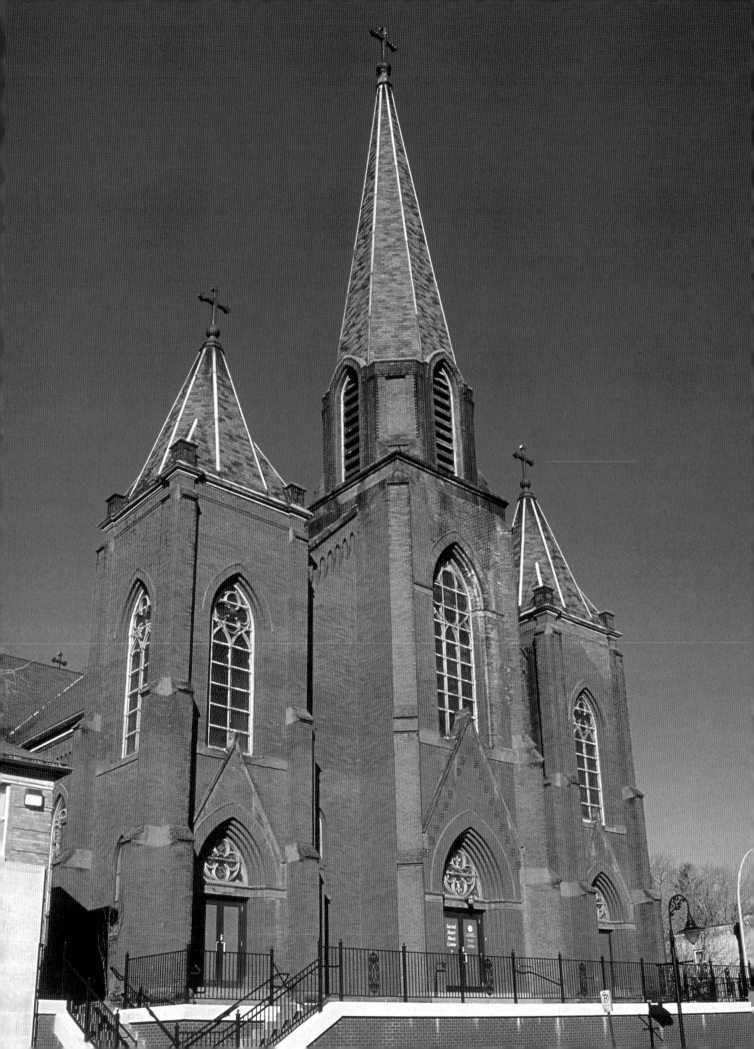

Arts Scene

A vital component to any community, the arts hold a celebrated position in the Twin Ports. A long history of support for music and theatre has created an outlet for many musicians and actors. The visual arts have also found fertile ground to flourish. Support for the arts is a tradition that has been valued and nurtured by the public schools and colleges in our area. A number of annual festivals dedicated to art, music and dance take place throughout the year in the Twin Ports.

The Depot/St. Louis County Heritage & Arts Center

The Arts Center has been an important incubator for many arts activities. Organizations like the Duluth Superior Symphony Orchestra, Arrowhead Chorale, Lake Superior Chamber Orchestra and Matinee Musicale have brought world classical music and musicians to the Twin Ports for decades.

Sacred Heart Music Center

Sacred Heart Music Center is known for its incredible acoustics. The building and its organ were saved from the wrecking ball by grassroots efforts. It is used for concerts, recording space and weddings.

Weber Music Hall

Opened in 2002, Weber Music Hall on the UMD campus is the newest venue in the Twin Ports. An intimate setting with tremendous acoustics, it is a great addition to UMD's music program.

Duluth Entertainment and Convention Center

The Duluth Entertainment and Convention Center (DECC), while it is a beautiful meeting space, offers quite a lot more. It has an auditorium, two ice rinks, exhibition space, ballrooms

Weber Music Hall

The DECC

overlooking the harbor and an OMNIMAX theater. The DECC even has eight "sheets" of ice for the Duluth Curling Club, which is one of the largest clubs in the United States. It can be expanded to 13 sheets for large tournaments (bonspiels).

Tweed Museum of Art at UMD

Tweed Museum of Art on the UMD campus hosts regular exhibitions throughout the year. It has an important permanent collection of over 4,000 pieces from around the world dating from the 15th century to the present. Collections include European art, American art, and the Glenn C. Nelson Ceramics Collection.

Coffeehouse and Gallery Scene

On any given weekend, musical performances from punk to jazz to folk can be heard at local coffeehouses and taverns. Many of these same establishments display artworks of all media by local artists. Art galleries flourish in Canal Park and the downtown shopping district.

Theater and Dance

Duluth is home to the Minnesota Ballet, one of the finest dance companies in the Midwest. Minnesota Ballet travels throughout the country and also internationally, performing a range of original works from classic ballet to jazz and modern dance. The School of Minnesota Ballet offers classes and performance opportunities for people of all ages and abilities.

All three of the Twin Ports' major educational institutions have thriving theater departments. Some productions include guest directors, and others are entirely managed by students. The Duluth Playhouse, in operation since 1914, presents several mainstage musicals and plays each season and also runs a Children's Theater. Comedy theater finds a warm welcome in Duluth; local troupes perform regularly.

Tweed Museum of Art at UMD

Parks & Natural Areas

Duluth's city parks include the usual athletic fields and picnic areas, but many have uniquely stunning natural features of streams and rocky outcrops. Downhill and cross-country skiing, golf courses, rock climbing, skating rinks and ball fields are found within the city limits. The area's wildlife regularly uses the many streams that flow down the hillside as natural corridors into our urban environment. It is not uncommon to hear of black bears eating apples or raiding trashcans in backyards. Moose occasionally stroll through neighborhoods.

Enger Tower

The observation tower, gardens and picnic grounds overlook the city from West Skyline Parkway. Upon his death, Bert Enger, a Norwegian immigrant, left funds for a tower to be built on land he had donated to the city. The tower was dedicated by Crown Prince Olav of Norway in 1939. On these grounds, Duluth celebrates its sister city, Ohara, Japan, with a peace garden.

Skyline Parkway

Stretching from one end of Duluth to the other, the Skyline Parkway gives the visitor spectacular vistas of the city, its historic neighborhoods and the natural splendor of the area. Beginning at Becks Road to the west and ending at Seven Bridges Road to the east, this scenic drive follows Duluth's ridgeline for 30 miles, with numerous places to stop for views, including Hawk Ridge. Seven Bridges Road descends along Amity Creek and the Lester River as they cascade over waterfalls to Lake Superior at 60th Avenue East.

The Willard Munger State Trail

The Munger Trail follows the former mainline of the Northern Pacific Railroad that was abandoned in the late 1970s. It was named for the Environmentalist and State Legislator Willard Munger of Duluth. The trail starts just off of Grand Avenue in

One of many streams flowing down Duluth's hillside

western Duluth, across from the Lake Superior Zoo, and goes all the way to Hinckley, MN. It is a popular trail for biking, hiking and inline skating.

Leif Erickson Park

On the Lakewalk west of the Rose Garden sits an outdoor amphitheater facing the Lake. It is a favorite spot for picnics, festivals and soaking up some sun. A full-size replica of the type of ship used by the Vikings calls this park home. This ship, the *Leif Erickson*, sailed across the Atlantic from Bergen, Norway, to Duluth in 1926.

Rose Garden

Come stroll or sit on a bench and enjoy the lakeview surrounded by more than 40,000 roses, including All-American Rose Selection winners. On London Road east of Leif Erickson Park, the Rose Garden was founded in 1967 by the Duluth Rose Society.

West Skyline Parkway overlooking the harbor

Seven Bridges Road (East Skyline Parkway), Lester Park

Superior, Wisconsin

Fairlawn Mansion

Overlooking the harbor on Route 53, this great Victorian mansion was built in 1889 by Superior's three-term mayor Martin Pattison. Now a museum open to the public, Fairlawn recalls the elegance and prosperity of Superior's early boomtown days, as well as the mansion's unique 42 years as a children's home.

Trails Galore

Superior has a number of excellent trails within the city limits. The Superior Municipal Forest is comprised of 4,500 lush acres of forest and natural habitat. During the winter, the forest boasts 26 kilometers of fine cross-country skiing. The trailhead is at 28th Street & Wyoming Avenue, and a seasonal or daily fee is charged. Skijoring—dog-assisted cross-country skiing—is allowed on a designated portion of the trail.

Seamen statue on Barker's Island

Superior Municipal Forest trail

Barker's Island

A delight and refuge for visitors and residents, Barker's Island hosts a full service marina, harbor tours, hotel and restaurants. Excellent trails, swimming and shopping make it a popular destination. The *S.S. Meteor*, the last remaining whaleback ship in the world, is permanently docked on Barker's Island. The annual Lake Superior Dragon Boat Festival is held in the Barker's Island Area, with proceeds from the event going to charities.

Richard I. Bong WWII Heritage Center

The aim of the Heritage Center is to educate about the lasting effects that WWII has on the way we live today. It is named for Richard Bong, who was born in Superior, Wisconsin. He earned the Congressional Medal of Honor for his skill and daring as a fighter pilot. The main exhibit is a restored P-38 plane.

Superior Port Entry

Built in 1913, the Wisconsin Point Lighthouse is situated at the natural outlet of the St. Louis River. The original equipment included a god signal and a Fourth-Order Fresnel Lens. The Wisconsin Point Lighthouse now uses an electric beacon.

Wisconsin Point Lighthouse at the Superior Port Entry

RICHARD I. BONG
WWII HERITAGE CENTER

Richard I. Bong WWII Heritage Center

Spring in Duluth

For many Duluthians, very specific signs signal the arrival of spring. For instance, the first ships to be ushered under the Aerial Lift Bridge means the beginning of the season of boatwatching—and bridged motorists. For water enthusiasts and fisherfolk, spring begins with iceout and the opening of the fishing season. The warmth of the spring sun brings the emergence of wildflowers and insects, and the arrival of loons and hummingbirds. Hawks return to familiar territories or pass through to northern breeding grounds. Hillsides full of lupine and hedges full of lilacs are eagerly anticipated treasures after the long winter. As the season gets more inviting, increasing numbers of joggers use the streets and the Lakewalk as they prepare for Grandma's Marathon in the summer. Walkers enjoy the lengthening daylight and soft spring nights on the Lakewalk. By the arrival of Memorial Day weekend, it is safe to make a garden. Eventually, the roller-coaster weather patterns of spring even out: it's time for summer.

Fishing along Lake Superior

Common Loon, Minnesota's state bird

Summer in Duluth

While the rest of the state will experience the distress of a humid, 80°F-plus day, a Duluthian basks comfortably, opening the windows to let in the cool, soft wind off Lake Superior. Known as the "air conditioned city," Duluth is the perfect oasis for the heat-intolerant Midwesterner to escape at least one climate extreme. To beat any summer heat wave, head for Lake Superior and dip in a toe, skip a few rocks or take a romantic evening stroll along the Lakewalk. Guaranteed, the closer one is to the Lake, the cooler the air. Most Duluthians agree, it's one good reason to live Up North.

In the spring and summer, Duluth literally blossoms. The Rose Garden in Leif Erickson Park and the gardens at Enger Tower are favorite locations for weddings. Duluth is also a golfer's paradise; numerous public and private golf courses evoke the irresistible urge to hit the links.

Major summer events include the Park Point Art Fair, Fourthfest, the Blues Festival and Grandma's Marathon. This remarkably scenic marathon course from Two Harbors to Duluth's Canal Park draws over 9,000 participants every June from around the world. Wednesday night sailboat races are another lovely tradition. But sailing isn't the only seafaring pastime; imagine any water sport and it is probably available in Duluth, from sea kayaking to charter fishing.

Grandma's Marathon

Enger Park Golf Course, West Skyline Parkway

<< **Rose Garden at Leif Erickson Park**

Fall in Duluth

With leaves changing colors under crisp blue skies, fall is a gorgeous time of year in Duluth. As the shipping season nears its end, salties rush to get one last load of grain to take overseas. Brisk nighttime temperatures bring ice to the inland lakes by Thanksgiving or early December. Gardeners put their vegetable and flower plots to bed, and bears raid the apple trees. Boaters take their boats out of the freezing lake and skiers prepare their equipment. Folks enjoy fall color tours along Duluth's North Shore Scenic Drive.

An annual September event in Duluth is the North Shore Inline Marathon: a great spectacle of 5,000 inline skaters skimming along the same 26.2-mile scenic course of Grandma's Marathon. It is the largest inline race in the world.

Hawk Ridge

Located on the easternmost segment of Skyline Parkway, bordering the Lester River, Hawk Ridge is one of the nation's best places to observe the annual raptor migrations. The first hawk watch was organized in 1951. Observation increased from a few days in mid-September to daily counts August through November, once the magnitude of the migration became apparent. In fact, the count at Hawk Ridge is one of the two or three highest in the continent. Visitors from all over the world arrive in Duluth to watch the hawks on their migration.

Other activities at Hawk Ridge include ongoing research, and public or group programs educating on subjects like hawk identification, migration and raptor biology.

North Shore Inline Marathon

Hawk Ridge birders

Winter in Duluth

This is the season many Duluthians wait for: a winter with lots of snow. Anticipation of the first snowfall builds as the days shorten and the temperatures drop. Around Thanksgiving, snowshoe hares grow a lovely new white fur coat and stand out like sore thumbs while they wait for the snow-cover. Depending on weather trends, Duluthians expect the first snowfall in October. Cold weather is easily addressed with a variety of outerwear, or "layering systems." Dressing for the weather can be a major fashion statement in the Northland. Getting around is not an issue; the City of Duluth street crews do a great job clearing away the snow. After sizeable seasonal accumulation, the "snow trains" run during the night to clear away snowbanks in business districts and primary intersections. Dump trucks following front-end loaders haul the snow away. Secretly, a lot of Duluthians look forward to the big snowstorm that shuts things down for a day, giving them time to run snow-blowers, make soup, bake cookies and finally get out to talk to the neighbors not seen since Halloween.

The Christmas City of the North Parade is a jumpstart to winter activities in late November. Duluthians are quickly deep into hockey—from the neighborhood outdoor rinks, to major competition of local high school and college teams playing at the DECC Arena. The UMD Bulldog Men's and Women's teams have been national champions and always draw huge crowds.

The finer art of Curling—a sport like shuffleboard on ice with brooms—is also hosted at the DECC. Olympic-caliber teams have been a tradition in Duluth.

The John Beargrease Sled Dog Marathon held mid- to late winter is a qualifier for the Alaskan Iditarod. The 400–mile race starts and finishes in Duluth. The route follows North Shore trails to the turn-around point north of Grand Marais. Spectators can visit checkpoints and participate in associated events. The event is named for John Beargrease, who carried mail in the late 1880s to the isolated communities along the North Shore. His fastest winter trip from Two Harbors to Grand Marais was 28 hours.

John Beargrease Sled Dog Marathon

Lake boat steams to its winter berth

Ski centers offering downhill, cross-country and skijumping facilities all are within minutes of downtown Duluth and Superior. Spirit Mountain has a number of ski runs and snowmaking equipment and is open around Thanksgiving. Most cross-country trails are public and groomed.

Even fisherfolk don't let a little ice stop them; great fishing is available almost year-round. Once there is enough ice to support them, little villages of ice fishing houses appear on lakes and rivers.

Christmas City of the North Parade

Snowboarding on Spirit Mountain

Ice fishing houses on the St. Louis River

From snowmobiling and skiing to ice fishing and snowshoeing, there's something for every wintersport enthusiast.

Conclusion

Raised on the flat farmland of Illinois, my husband Tim and I came to live on the North Shore of Lake Superior for all the visions you find in this book. We came to seek the fulfillment of a lifelong goal to live near wilderness, a major port for ships and trains, incredible clear water and a broad horizon. Consciously or unconsciously, I think we all have a spot inside of us that defines our personal geography. It may be the plains, hills, trees or a certain horizon that make us feel like we are home, giving us comfort. Sometimes these are features we seek as we plan for a new adventure or vacation because they aren't like what we're used to.

We've raised our children here as Duluthians, Minnesotans and outdoor enthusiasts. We never take for granted everything this area has to offer, both in its present state and in the deeper levels of intriguing history that characterizes Duluth. Tim and I found in Duluth an exciting adventure and a place to call home, as well as that defining element of personal identity, all things worth passing down to the next generations.

Anita Zager

Ellen and John tobogganing

BIBLIOGRAPHY

Aubut, Sheldon T. and Maryanne C. Norton. *Duluth, Minnesota: Images of America*. Chicago, IL: Arcadia, 2001.

Benson, David R. *Stories in Log and Stone: The Legacy of the New Deal in Minnesota State Parks*. St. Paul, MN: State of Minnesota, Department of Natural Resources, Division of Parks and Recreation, 2002.

Frederick, Chuck. *Duluth: The City and The People*. Helena, MT: American & World Geographic Publishing, 1994.

Germ, Mary Lou. *Duluth: Past to Present*. Ashland, WI: Paradigm Press, 1977.

Gilman, Rhoda R. *The Story of Minnesota's Past*. St. Paul, MN: Minnesota Historical Society Press, 1989.

Green, John. *Geology on Display: Geology and Scenery of Minnesota's North Shore State Parks*. St. Paul, MN: State of Minnesota, Department of Natural Resources, 1996.

Hyde, Charles K. *The Northern Lights: Lighthouses of The Upper Great Lakes*. Detroit, MI: Wayne State University Press, 1986.

LeLievre, Roger, ed. *Know Your Ships 2003*. Sault Ste Marie, MI: Marine Publishing Company, 2003.

Lydecker and Sommer, ed. *Duluth: Sketches of the Past, City of Duluth*. Duluth, MN: City of Duluth, American Bicentennial Commission, 1976.

Marshall, Jim, ed. *Shipwrecks of Lake Superior*. Duluth, MN: Lake Superior Magazine, 1987.

Miller, Al. *Tin Stackers: The History of the Pittsburgh Steamship Company*. Detroit, MI: Wayne State University, 1999.

Morton, Ron and Carl Gawboy. *Talking Rocks*. Duluth, MN: Pfeifer-Hamilton, 2000.

Peacock, Thomas and Marlene Wisuri. *Ojibwe: Waasa Inaabidaa—We Look in All Directions*. Afton, MN: Afton Historical Society Press, 2002.

Roots in the Past—Seeds for the Future: The Heritage & History of Clover Valley, French River & Surrounding Communities. Duluth, MN: Clover Valley, French River Community History Committee, North Shore Elementary School, 2000.

Sandvik, Glenn N. *Duluth: An Illustrated History of the Zenith City*. Eugene, OR: Windsor Publications, 1983.

Scott, James, John Ulven and Robert Calton. *Duluth's Legacy, Volume 1: Architecture*. Edited by Gerald M. Kimball. Duluth, MN: City of Duluth, Dept of Research & Planning, 1974.

Young, Frank A. *Duluth's Ship Canal and Aerial Bridge: And How They Came To Be*. Duluth, MN: Stewart-Taylor Company, 1977.

America's Byways
www.byways.org

City of Superior, Wisconsin
www.ci.superior.wi.us

Citysearch: Duluth, Minnesota
http://duluth.citysearch.com

College of St. Scholastica
www.css.edu

Duluth Convention and Visitors Bureau
www.visitduluth.com

Duluth Entertainment Convention Center
www.decc.org

Duluth News Tribune
www.duluthsuperior.com

Duluth Seaway Port Authority
www.duluthport.com

Duluth Shipping News
www.duluthshippingnews.com

John Beargrease Sled Dog Marathon
www.beargrease.com

Minnesota Historical Society
www.mnhs.org

R. J. Houle Visitor Information Center
www.lakecnty.com

Superior-Douglas County Convention and Visitors Bureau
www.visitsuperior.com

University of Minnesota Duluth
www.d.umn.edu

University of Wisconsin Superior
www.uwsuper.edu

INDEX

Aerial Lift Bridge 37
agates 15
architecture 81–87
Arthur P. Cook House 86
airports 73

Barker's Island 110
Bayfront Festival Park 99

Canal Park 97
College of St. Scholastica (CSS) 76
Copper Top Church *see First United Methodist Church*

Depot 81–82, 101
Duluth Entertainment and Convention
    Center (DECC) 101–2
Duluth International Airport 73
Duluth Playhouse 103
Duluth Port Entry Lighthouses 51
Duluth Public Library 85
Duluth Ship Canal 33–34

Enger Tower 105

Fairlawn Mansion 109
First United Methodist Church 84
fishing, commercial 57
Fitger's 82–84
Fond du Lac 23
fur trade 23, 25, 29

Glensheen 82
Gooseberry Falls State Park 54
Great Lakes Aquarium (GLA) 94

Hawk Ridge 15, 117
Henry H. Meyers House 86
hospitals 79

iron ore 61

Jay Cooke State Park 17–18
John Beargrease Sled Dog Marathon 119

Kitchi Gammi Club 85

Lake Superior 13, 29–30, 43
Lake Superior Maritime Visitor Center 93
Lake Superior Railroad Museum 95
Lake Superior Tugboat 94
Lake Superior Zoo 93
Lakewalk 99
Leif Erickson Park 106
lighthouses 49–53, 110
lumber 67

Miller-Dwan Medical Center 79
Minnesota Ballet 102
Minnesota Point 21
Minnesota Point Lighthouse 49–51

north pier light 51
North Shore 53–55
North Shore Scenic Railroad 95

Observation Hill 86
Ojibwe 23, 25
Old Duluth Central High School 81

parks 105–7
portages 30

railroading 63–65
Richard I. Bong WWII Heritage Center 110
Rose Garden 106

S. S. Meteor 59
S. S. William A. Irvin Ore Boat Museum 94
Sacred Heart Music Center 101
schools 75-77, 81
sculpture 91
shipping 29–30, 33–34, 41, 49, 59, 69–71
shipwrecks 47
Sky Harbor Airport 73
Skyline Parkway 15, 105
Split Rock Lighthouse 53
St. Louis County Heritage &
    Arts Center 81–82, 99
St. Louis River 17
St. Luke's Hospital 79
St. Mary's/Duluth Clinic (SMDC) 79
statistics 11
Sundew Coast Guard Cutter 95
Superior, Wisconsin 17, 109–11

topography 15
Tweed Museum of Art (UMD) 102
Two Harbors' Agate Bay 54
Two Harbors Lighthouse 53

University of Minnesota Duluth (UMD) 75–76
University of Wisconsin Superior (UWS) 76

Vista Fleet 94

waterfront 21, 97
weather 43
Weber Music Hall (UMD) 101
Willard Munger State Trail 105–6
Wisconsin Point Lighthouse 110